Farmer Will Allen

and the

GROWING TABLE

WRITTEN BY **Jacqueline Briggs Martin**

ILLUSTRATED BY **Eric-Shabazz Larkin**

AFTERWORD BY WILL ALLEN

Readers
to **Eaters**

BELLEVUE, WASHINGTON

Readers *to* Eaters

READERS to EATERS Books
12437 SE 26th Place, Bellevue, WA 98005
Distributed by Publishers Group West

www.ReadersToEaters.com

Printed in the U.S.A. by Worzalla, Stevens Point, Wisconsin (5/13)

Book design by Red Herring Design

Book production by The Kids at Our House

The text is set in Walden Font Co. Civil War Press Type No. 1, based on typography found on recruitment posters and other printed material of the era.

The art is done in ink and pen, and markers to make an image or color, then digitally matched with scanned textures and objects.

Photograph of Will Allen on page 31 by Darren Hauck
Photographs of Growing Power on pages 31-32 by Vera Chang

10 9 8 7 6 5 4 3 2 1
First Edition

Library of Congress Control Number: 2013937817
ISBN 978-0-9836615-3-5

To all those who've ever planted a seed and watched it grow—
farmers who tend food and flowers and tend the earth. —J.B.M.

To my God that gave me this body.
To my parents that fed it well.
To my wife that made it happy. —E.-S.L.

Farmer Will Allen is as tall as his truck.
He can hold a cabbage—or a basketball—in one hand.
When he laughs, everyone laughs, glad to be in his crew.
When he talks, everyone listens.

But some say the special thing about Will Allen

is that HE CAN SEE WHAT OTHERS CAN'T SEE.

Are they right?
When he looked at an abandoned city lot
and saw a huge table heaped with food, was he right?

When Will Allen was a boy
bowls of peas, greens,
and his favorite—lima beans with ham—
covered the kitchen table.

"My mother often fixed enough food for thirty," Will says.
"We never had a car or a TV, but we always had good food."
He remembers people who'd come to dinner
tired and drooped—
and leave LAUGHING.

Will's family grew most of their food.
Will loved the food but hated the work.

He planned to quit on PLANTING,
PICKING, PULLING WEEDS,
leave those Maryland fields for
basketball or white-shirt work.

And he did.
He graduated from college
and moved to Belgium to
play professional

BASKETBALL.

When a Belgian friend asked him
   to help dig potatoes
Will realized he "loved digging in the dirt."
HE GREW SO MUCH FOOD
that he and his wife Cyndy covered
   their kitchen table
with Thanksgiving dinner for
a team of basketball friends.

When Will was done with basketball,
he worked a white-shirt job in Wisconsin
and found time to grow vegetables
on Cyndy's parents' land.

But Will wanted his own place.
He'd seen that fresh vegetables
were as scarce in the city
as trout in the desert.
Will believed everyone, everywhere,
had a **RIGHT** to good food.

BUT HOW could Will farm
in the middle of pavement and parking lots?

One day, driving in Milwaukee,
Will spotted six empty greenhouses
on a plot of land about the size of a large supermarket,
FOR SALE!

He could see kids,
who'd never eaten a ripe tomato,
never crunched a raw green bean,
sitting at his table, eating his vegetables.
Will Allen bought that city lot!

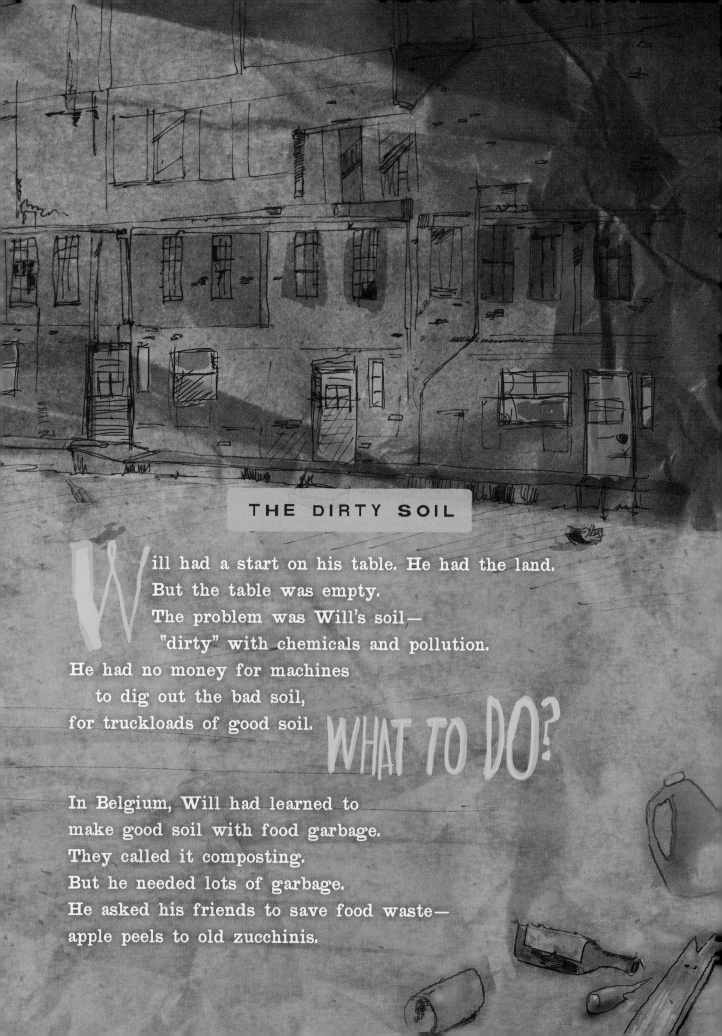

THE DIRTY SOIL

Will had a start on his table. He had the land.
But the table was empty.
The problem was Will's soil—
    "dirty" with chemicals and pollution.
He had no money for machines
    to dig out the bad soil,
for truckloads of good soil.

WHAT TO DO?

In Belgium, Will had learned to
make good soil with food garbage.
They called it composting.
But he needed lots of garbage.
He asked his friends to save food waste—
apple peels to old zucchinis.

Will collected those scraps in big white buckets
and dumped them into piles.

He added
        hay,
            leaves,
                newspapers,
                    red wiggler WORMS,
                        water.

Every now and then he turned the piles
to get air into the mix.
Neighborhood kids stopped by to ask what he was doing.

Will told them about the piles
and the red wiggler worms
that would help the garbage become compost.
The kids came back day after day to help.

RED WIGGLER WORMS

Then one day—bad news:

THE RED WIGGLER CREW WAS DYING.

Will and the kids studied worms for five years.
They learned not to feed the worms too much.
And they discovered the best menu for red wigglers:
    no hot peppers, onions, garlic;
    lots of watermelon rinds, sweet potato scraps, molasses.
Since then the squirmy crew has stayed hard at work.
Will says worm "magic" is what makes his farm grow.

Once Will had good soil,
he was ready to plant vegetables.
But he didn't have much space.
How could he GROW ENOUGH FOOD
on a small city plot?

Will Allen looked around.
He saw that he had *all* the space
from the soil under his feet
to the top of the greenhouses.

He hung plant baskets from the ceiling.
He grew greens in buckets, greens in rows.
He crowded shelves with pots of spinach, chard, lettuce.
He grew stacks of tiny salad sprouts
in boxes, hundreds of boxes.

Will added hoophouses to hold more boxes
and more long rows of vegetables.
He added vats of water and fish to his greenhouses.
Fish wastewater grows the sprouts.
The sprouts clean the water for the fish.
FISH, WATER, SPROUTS
WORK TOGETHER
like a three-part FARM MACHINE.

He added goats, chickens, turkeys, and bees
to that city farm he named "Growing Power."

Farmer Will's work clothes
are jeans and a blue sweatshirt
    with cutoff sleeves.
    He's busy from early morning to night.
Still, one person could never grow all the food Will wanted to grow.
Where could he find more farmers in the middle of the city?

Will Allen looked around.
He saw teenagers, schoolchildren, parents, grandparents.

HE TAUGHT THEM TO BE FARMERS.

Then Will's "table" held as much as several supermarkets—
thousands of pounds of food.

Neighbors who live in high-rises,
far off the growing ground,
came—and still come—to Will's farm
to buy fresh vegetables, fish, or eggs.
People have gone—and still go—
to fancy restaurants to eat Will's food.

But Will wanted his table to feed folks all over the world.
How could he build one **HUGE** table that crossed continents?

Will thought about the problem
of the world-sized table.
He looked around and saw his many helpers
who'd learned to be farmers.
He would teach people EVERYWHERE
to grow food for
their own tables.

Will Allen began to travel.
He has crisscrossed the United States
showing others how to farm in the city.
And he has taken his red wigglers to Kenya,
to London— ALL OVER THE WORLD.

The world has also come to his Milwaukee farm.
Twenty thousand visitors a year
tour the greenhouses, watch goats, snack on greens,
and go home planning to START A FARM on a city lot,
rooftop, or abandoned highway.

Is Will Allen done? NEVER!

"We need fifty million more people growing food
on porches, in pots, in side yards," he says.
Will is always looking for
new ways to make the table bigger—
more schoolyard plots,
a vertical farm that's five stories high,
farms in empty factories or warehouses.

Will Allen dreams of a day when city farms
are as common as streetlights,
and EVERY TABLE IS
COVERED WITH GOOD FOOD.

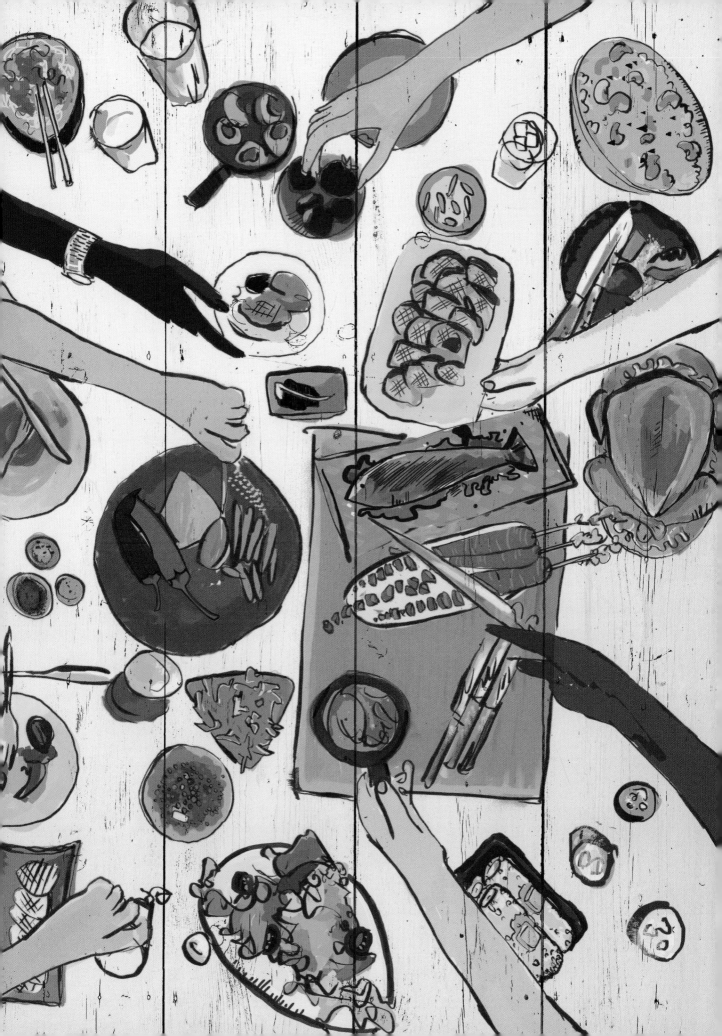

Will Allen can see
what others can't see.
When he sees kids,
he sees farmers.

Will you be on Will Allen's crew?
Will you grow vegetables
for your family, your neighbors,
on your porch, or roof, or yard?

How big will YOUR table be?

GROWING POWER INC.

Dear Reader, Eater, maybe Future Farmer—

I am glad we are able to meet through this book.

As you know, I did not want to farm when I was young, but now I love growing food that tastes good. I like to farm in all sorts of places. Sometimes I have gardens in the ground, like a garden in your backyard. Sometimes I like to put gardens on roofs or hang my plants from hangers on small pipes. My next big project is to build a tall building. It will not be full of offices or apartments, but will be filled with lots of plants—fresh salad greens, tomatoes and other vegetables.

I'm very pleased you are learning about farming, about growing and eating good, healthy food. I hope you know that you are the key to helping people, at home and around the world, have better, safer and healthier food to eat. How?

1. By eating lots of fresh veggies and fruits.

2. By planting your own small garden anywhere—in your backyard or front lawn, on your porch or deck, in pots in your kitchen or in your living room. You could even put a garden in your bedroom and grow good food for yourself and your family!

3. By starting a worm factory! That's right.... I said WORMS, because worms are great! The secret to being a great farmer is great soil to farm in. Start a compost bin with your parents and get those worms working.

Finally, I invite you to visit my Growing Power farm in Milwaukee, Wisconsin, and bring your parents and friends along too. We would love to show you all the things we have growing in our greenhouses.... including our livestock— the red wiggler worms.

I can't wait to see what you grow.

WILL ALLEN
Farmer, Founder and CEO, Growing Power, Inc.

I grew up on a dairy farm in Maine. We always had a huge garden. And, like Will Allen, I did not like garden work. The rows seemed so long and the sun so hot.

However, since becoming an adult, I have planted seeds in pots, buckets, small patches of ground, and I love stories of growing food and flowers—and especially stories of growing food and flowers in unlikely places—such as cities.

That is why I am very happy to be able to tell the story of Will Allen. His work at Growing Power has revolutionized urban farming. Thousands have learned from him how to grow food using raised beds, fish-farming—even "worm-farming" with the hardworking red wiggler worms. He has taught city farmers to make tons of compost using food waste generated in cities. And he has shown that urban farms can be the source of good jobs for underemployed urban residents. In addition to the Milwaukee farm, Growing Power actively assists other urban farmers all over the world.

For his work he was given a MacArthur "Genius Grant" in 2008 and the Theodore Roosevelt Award, the highest honor given by the National Collegiate Athletic Association in 2012.

Will Allen's life reminds us of the power of one person with a vision.

—JACQUELINE BRIGGS MARTIN

RESOURCES

You can grow many kinds of plants in buckets or pots. Or you can grow a plastic sack farm. Here are some good reads to help you get started:

Bucklin-Sporer, Arden & Pringle, Rachel. *How to Grow a School Garden: A Complete Guide for Parents and Teachers.* Portland, OR: Timber Press, 2010.

Fleischman, Paul. *Seedfolks.* New York: HarperTeen, 1997.

Fox, Thomas. *Urban Farming.* Lexington, KY: Hobby Farm Press, 2011.

French, Vivian. *Yucky Worms.* Illustrated by Jessica Ahlberg. Cambridge, MA: Candlewick, 2010.

Hendy, Jenny. *The Ultimate Step-by-Step Kids' First Gardening Book.* Leicester, England: Lorenz Books, 2010.

Krezel, Cindy & Curtis, Bruce. *Kids' Container Gardening: Year-Round Projects for Inside and Out.* Chicago: Chicago Review Press, 2010.

Lovejoy, Sharon. *Roots, Shoots, Buckets & Boots: Gardening Together With Children.* New York: Workman, 1999.

McGee, Rose Marie Nichols & Stuckey, Maggie. *McGee & Stuckey's Bountiful Container.* New York: Workman Publishing, 2002.

Neville, Jayne. *Flowerpot Farming.* Preston, UK: Good Life Press, 2008.

Pfeffer, Wendy. *Wiggling Worms at Work.* Illustrated by Steve Jenkins. New York: HarperCollins, 2003.

Swann, Rick. *Our School Garden.* Illustrated by Christy Hale. Bellevue, Washington: Readers to Eaters, 2012.

Waters, Alice. *Edible Schoolyard: A Universal Idea.* San Francisco: Chronicle Books, 2008.

To learn more about Will Allen, read his autobiography, *The Good Food Revolution: Growing Healthy Food, People, and Communities.* (Gotham Books, 2012), or go to www.growingpower.org. For a complete list of my references, go to the book's web page at www.readerstoeaters.com/books/will-allen-and-the-growing-table. —J.B.M.

Jacqueline Briggs Martin has written numerous award-winning children's books, including *Snowflake Bentley*, winner of the Caldecott Medal. Her other honors include American Library Association's Notable List, the Golden Kite Award, and Maine Lupine Award. She grew up on a farm in Maine and now lives in Mt. Vernon, Iowa. Learn more about Jacqueline at jacquelinebriggsmartin.com.

Eric-Shabazz Larkin is a multi-disciplinary fine artist and film maker. He is also the founder of Creative School of Thought, a production studio for art and film works geared to social change. He lives in New York City. This is his first book for children. Learn more about Eric at www.creativeschoolofthought.com.